OPTIC OPENING

sejal akerkar

Copyright © 2022 Sejal Akerkar All rights reserved

The poems portrayed in this collection are based on personal thoughts and experiences. Any similar feelings towards real persons are not coincidental and not intended by the author.

No part of this book may be reproduced, or stored in a retrieval system, or transmitted in any form or by any means, electronic, mechanical, photocopying, recording, or otherwise, without express written permission of the publisher.

Cover Illustration by: Sejal Akerkar

this book is dedicated to my aji, a woman who believed in me from every sideline. thank you for teaching me how to be strong in more ways than one. may your soul find rest until we meet again. i love you.

beneficiary

all of the proceeds from this book will be donated to Udayan Care, a non-profit organization. they strive to improve the lives of orphaned and abandoned children and provide education and mentoring to poor girls in india. my family has been associated with Udayan Care for eleven years. we have visited and celebrated with them. my first poetry collection is still currently helping support them. the connections i had with some of the girls and their stories at Udayan Care still inspire me to donate the proceeds of my collection to them and their fellow sisters and brothers. these donations will help educate the children of Udayan Care and allow them to express themselves in society like i am.

contents

my dictionary 3

respite 23

rationalization 49

reclamation 87

restore 119

raw 153

dear… 183

as your eyes devour my words on the right side, allow your thoughts to spill on to the left. those pages are empty for you. please dump your intrusive opinions and perceptions. they're dying to listen. enjoy.

greetings to the end of the book

hello over there

so many pages away

a journey unfolded

there at the end you lay

i hope it was well worth it

being the end of the book

stolen the show

like a criminal or a crook

you are greatly appreciated

as am i

to wrap up a culmination

opening up eyes

i've heard great things

how was the ride

i guess you can tell me

see you on the other side

my dictionary

petrichor

(n) are you able to feel an aroma

the smell of earth

soil quenching thirst

by the downpour from above

a fresh aftertaste

to wash all our footprints away

we stand hand in hand

with the dampness of rain

revitalize our soul

for all the storms we've left behind

eccedentesiast

(n) you try to believe that a grin

will hide your sadness

but your teeth fall out when you smile

because pain rots them away

hiraeth

(n) mars isn't far enough

for us to inhabit with

our inescapable curse

yearning of our braved oceans

leaving our comfort lands

we reach a point where

we can't find home

in homesickness

we ruin this world

until we have to run from it

humdudgeon

(n) a sickness infests her brain

only mind's way of imaginary

lies an illness with no physical

attributes seeping from her insides

fingers tremble to the slightest touch

even when still

still diagnosed an imaginary illness

kalopsia

(n) she sees you for who you are

a broken record just needing some tape

delusional of the scratchy tunes

tranquilly humming to your flaws

believing things are more beautiful

than they really are

mizpah

(n) the only larger feeling than love, is loss

i can feel your bond through his tears

separated by lifetimes

holding onto each other

through a time warp dimension

you're ripping the seam

please sew it back together

patches of your lives fill conjoining quilts

before the time machine breaks

turn the loss back to love

for him please

phosphenes

(n) sailing down on earth

touch it with your feet

don't be disrespectful, but go ahead

i won't judge floating one

battling the tides of gravity just to move the sun

rubbing your eyes to view live stars

is the loneliness of an astronaut

nefelibata

(n) intertwined souls

i don't believe in love if

you can't read her thoughts on her palm

a cloud walker without a hand to hold

a palm reader without a hand to hold

agape

(n) on the pyramid of love

you are at the top

an incomplete triangle

strongest shape

of them all

faces measured

by the volume of your heart

because love

has too many faces

you believe that anger

means love

while others hold onto praise

tapping through options

for the universe

to read which what

you need

not the one you want

respite

perceptual feeling

if you found a forbidden forest

where would you run first

to a tree where you would

wood grabbing onto the creases of your hand

is where you would know

that we can never shade ourselves from the tree

that fell to never make a sound

happy birthday

closed eyes to candles

through time

days blend into each other

i wish to live life

truly live

feel the edges of death keeping

my eyelids open

confetti on my pillow celebrating

that slumber smile for once

pen stops seeping invisible ink

i only exist to the end of

my time

nothing else to write

wishes come true

where does happiness come from?

from long hugs where your heart beats sync

from the smell of rain

to three small words

the first sip of midnight water

or waking to snow

simple smiles through extended calls

dancing to music living through decades

sun on skins too beautiful

being alone

your favorite person's smell or

old polaroid's falling timely from the wall

the perfect glide of a pen and

a wagging tail

the glimmer in their eyes

and the new jar of creamy peanut butter

early flights to paradise

escaping along forbidden roads

warm showers with a good cry

    to know you can still feel sadness

for a grand piano

    to play every key

she still smiles

just for the little things

our scrapbook

memories seep from her eyes

and down her cheek

tasting her happy tears

made of wistful water

imprinted into the albums of her life

as she scrolls through forgotten years

which photos does she look at

after we take them

already in defeat

you might not know what to choose

believe that it will be okay

put some of that weight on your future self to figure out

a long jog always beats a fast sprint

it might seem like everything relies on this moment

but believe that you've got plenty more hurdles ahead

because when you don't know where you're going

any road will get you there

the theatre

a spotlight does the opposite of what it thinks it's doing

it only shines a brighter light on the shadows behind

life wouldn't give you your lead role without a stage crew

cherish the ones dressed in black

comfort body

i wish i could embrace

every negativity

out of me

i hug my knee

because sometimes

the only comfort i can find

is myself

hyperventilation

take a deep breathe

when you feel anxious

people say

breathing has now overwhelmed me

into suffocation

pen pals

was the love between

the sun

and the moon

moon controlling waves

sun controlling fauna

far but close enough

ruling existence

to draw stars across their sky

were their love letters

xoxo

wrote the sun in shooting star

you can see my dark side

replied the moon in meteor

moksha

when i look at my life behind me

and the one unwritten ahead of me

i take a thought to wonder

what lives am i missing out on

by living this one?

what joys are out of my grasp

is sadness nonexistent, unlike here

are there other dimensions of love and loss

that my body is not capable of intaking

is that other life

the finale

the stage where people are allowed

to take their final bow

to be granted freedom

in a world of chains and whips

is what my imagination dreams of

when i exist in this world

of terror and injustice and strife

i long to breath equal air

for the burning of the world

to be restored in my hands

i long to live in a place

of ultimate surrender

rationalization

heaven or hell

you feel like you should be in a place

that you've been asked to enter in

but have never seen

let me in

where do we love from? i love

from my smile. if i like you

i smile. some people love from their feet. towards another

to show attention. giving attention doesn't

always mean love. or does it. i wouldn't

know. as a young person.

i never know what to let go. and how

to let in. i will love your feet. or attention. whatever

you give. cause i'm desperate.

please.

want vs. need

we choose to let in what we want

because we are blinded to what we need

life has given us the task of evolving the difference

between our callings and our craves

we learn how to tear the blindfold

molding hands as decades role by

it becomes too late when we realize

that we could've tore it off all along

because inside we actually do know what we need

we just believe that what we want is more important

mid-century mahogany

sitting in a wooden cupboard

able to see the world behind glassed cabinets

you became my world

we were alone together and called it love

believing i didn't even deserve you

even when you were the only one i could see

cracking and chipping

delicate china gone bad

spoiled rotten

we accept the love we think we deserve

i gave you my pieces

to stand taller than any vase

to reverse any rottenness every cast upon you

i helped you heal

but in the process, it broke me

to see you throw your shadow stench

back in my face

you'd ruin my delicate china's grace

to predict nebulous years ahead

has she given up on life

or just let go of reality

so, she can't

tell the difference

between

hell or a fever dream

rushing to get through

that she never noticed

colors switched to gray

slowly fading from blue

can she change the sky with her eyes

or can the clouds just read her mind

morphed reflection

you see a question mark

a future so blurry

even glasses couldn't fix

the uncertainty seen in your eyes

she sees a human

someone breathing to live

while you're living to breath

in a world that doesn't show you

the right side of the mirror

looming loss

i agree, i think that falling out of love only hurts because you never know if the next one will be capable of treating you better.

these years

i am an orphan of the future

i can never seem to imagine a stable

hereafter ahead of me

envisions are blank

as i drive down these constant lanes

never knowing the answers

memories of my childhood pass through my youthful sleeves

gripping the steering wheel of life with naïve

ensuing paths of adulthood appear

but ever too tangled for me to compellingly

untangle

once upon a time: the villain's version

in this fairytale

the story doesn't end the way you've been told it should

somehow the villain gets the happily ever after in this one

because you always believe the other side's the villain

and never realize it's always been you

beyond the urn

you left with the last bindi

the last of the third eye

i was concealed from your wisdom

belated opening of the sixth chakra

i know you kept the key

and now it's too late for you to show me

where you've hidden it

hare or tortoise

she walks when

i can't run any longer

talks when my voice

has given into singing

skips even when my legs are

limp from leaping

keeps on reading when

my eyes roll back from memorizing

slower yet faster

she always wins the race

my closed doors

unfortunately

clothing can't dress my insides

to cover up my secrets

on my lips for never speaking up for myself

on my arms for being embarrassed

to raise them to all

never letting them be seen

on my knuckles for never fighting back

trying to swallow my closet

just so that nothing will be able to be on display

out-of-the-way

i meant that everyone feels love

all the time. not that it's towards someone

for eternity. but just the lust that you will

feel in the future. even when your hand

hasn't grown yet to reach it

karma

a game you never want to lose

someone deciding what's right

writing our past lives forward

who knows what edition you're playing

favored ones always getting the clues

two-wheeler

is love an instinct

or does it enhance over experience

like riding a bike

you have to be scared at first

to never know when they'll let you go

but most importantly

having to push the pedals to actually start going

kindling

just a little twinkle

could fuel a fire at any moment

i agree that you can fall out of love

but we will always feel it

outsider's aphasia

it resists translation

the words that others will never know

the ones that a translator stumbles on with their broken words

how do i explain this one?

with mismatched adjectives and confused ears

this one will never make sense

because you have to live in the word to really define it

reclamation

model minority

does intelligence radiate off the color of my skin

or can you just smell it?

the wafts of my unrealistic expectations

stinking up your american dream

manifest destiny

to sit on the lap of the angel

marching west

is to ignore the overlap of

america's attempt to push the world aside

original's beings stripped of their native label

others caged in ceaseless labor

outside faces fighting imperial powers

powers of abominable inspiration

slapped faces pulled to the hand of the growing nation

the ignorant hands

digging graves throughout the new land

burying immigrants with every spare moment

at chance

perishable engraved into their worn-out backs

backs that carry this country

towards centuries ahead

all forever victims of america

self-loathing

glancing at her reflection

impersonating her every move

was a girl she never knew

a girl she never wanted to see again

shattering the mirror to share the glass

with every inch of her body

she sits on the windowpane

pain gushing through her bones

she stabbed herself with herself

to hurt the person

she hated most

battle of the blues

can the strongest win

when the killer's on the loose

does the ocean's boundary

stop as she meets the

lips of land or does

she rush in to exclaim

that's the difference

between a blue whale and

a killer one

arranged marriage

and as a soul lusting

for love dies

dye stains her palms red

of henna falsified from it's

true form

marks another tally for

another perishable bond formed

washed up

the sand is trying to tell our history

through the broken glass shards

choking on our footprints

and strangling the voice of lost shores

hereditary hatred

even as we live away

we remember

generations inherit the same sinking revenge

for a people who sank us

forming a steel knife

to slash a wooden sword

their train churning

on our tracks

tore down our palaces

bare hands

belonging to thieves

of the world's greatest wonders

never able to repay

the livelihoods

they stole from us

photoshopped doom

our skin match to pixels

turning heads and heels

but never, to heal

the constant bashing of

everything labeled imperfect

airport security

a place where

the world should be checked equally

but metal detectors somehow see color

nations leaving baggage behind

to enter in a society

where the archway is built by

the bricks of racism

unapproachable from the outside

words hurt harder than hands

you want to lift your hand

to burn my face red

but instead, you use it to unzip your mouth

i can tell with the way diction writes your words

that you'd rather clench your fist

than unclench your jaw

cold war

staying silent doesn't erase spoken

movements leave blood

on the rope of tug of war

mortality remnant on both sides

because silence is never one sided

her satin dress

with the ability

to mellow down piles of flowers

laying in the juices of

the last rose

she was brought down

through glimmering

coffins and

colonized soil

dug up by men

red was her favorite color

as was his

she flew for his attention

for one sparkle of a glance

she floated in the rosy juices

and he just licked her joy

up dry

bone dry

may i meet dawn?

legs scared of each other

never knowing where they grew

searching and reaching

for a home in the soil

just to feel déjà vu

longing and limp

towards the ever-aging earth

ripping steps

sworn into battle

between home and the potential of the sky

fists of anchors

set on the victory

underneath to which they grow

to never fly

screams their angels

i will send you down where you only

knew the sound of worms

chomping on fresh souls

to where you heard prairies

sing in a place that feels like

where heaven is supposed

to be

the sun's ray's pin

your hands to topsoil

fresh enough to translate

your blood into your real desires

a body too heavenly

to ignore commands

the sun's angels send you down

toward the devil unearthed

exclaiming

behind its mask of dusk that

dawn has forced this new beginning

restore

polaroid

moments being captured live

forever on this wall

ones that need remembering

people who could be forgotten

in a year or two

many lost

the oxygen

sucked in and out

through the chest

hitting my veins

cutting my ribs

swallowing people and

places just to end up

at the very depth of my

stomach searching for

memories that only some can swim to

to become sickly sticky

and receive my implicit give

foreign exchange

polishing every outcome

that will finally

make them proud

trying to buy the sacrifice they paid

willing to forever

strive to give back the love

of country they lost

for us

all skin and bone

my brother could never

chase me through the

garden because he

failed to bloom

days flapped through

my hair

as the dirt

decided it's day to sail

was when we pit

ourselves against

each other as if

god didn't mold us all with

the same hands

disharmonies

can you ever let yourself be peaceful

in an unpeaceful world?

when will serenity

table chaos?

library's life story

books are timeless except

in a world where

conscious and mind are separate

one sees white

while the other sees black

do the words float around

a page

swimming through chapters

halted by

punctuation

or do they calculate formulas

plugging in spaces

where letters don't know

what to search for

even i, kill the birds and the trees

we stand vulnerable

next to our conflicting nations

on the same whereabouts

to fly into ungoverned waters

and breath in free air

stolen from the birds and the trees

my mind offered me too many thoughts

and not enough pages to contain them

overloaded ink with missing cartridges

learning to soak in silence

bruised fingers bowing to typing hands

even though i know now

only quills make the birds fly

i want to release doves with my words

pen strokes flapping through pages

turning every page with an axe

knowing that's what trees faced

just to be told what is written on them

forests don't deserve my oil spill

maternal vow

we never realize we stop growing

our mothers can't lift our gaze from their umbilical cords anymore

we forget that our one body is actually made up of two souls

sacrifice

always reveling in what could be

and not what we are set on

the path to build our own road

tiles laid next to their sacrifices

how do we live up

to what they left behind?

or can one day

we learn how to restore used tiles

into new futures untold

convincing them

that it was all worth it

coral

the swim of a fish

has the same impact

as a colossal wave

on the fraying hair of the pacific

collapse to colorless

woven through gashes

of the planet's unknown

engulfed in scum birthed from

under the fingernails of man

trial run

well that depends. you have to find what love is

not, to realize what it is

given up

i drag my heart on a leash

been shattered for

too long

i've just never looked in the mirror and

asked her to fix it

horizonless

i've searched so

long for the sun

that i've forgotten

what shade

tastes like

ancestors

we pass down our wings through generations

winged heirlooms

because even as they flew, we fought

fought feathered swords

knowing they're guarding your grip

eyes watching you grow

there even when we feel lost

and we bow our heads

not to the clouds resting above us but

to who flies beyond them

ode to animals

peace comes from

the disappearance of humans

when we leave, they

will finally be able to

listen to silence

a sound we will never be able to hear

the silence of the human hush

is the sound of

peace balancing the scales

of every ear drum ever damaged from our existence

hammering at cracked faces

only to be left with mouths

unable to scream

pulling at vocal strings

for every other being's lives

that matter too

raw

untitled #1

we ground our feet into the footholds of our ancestors

streamline

dropped to this country

their cartoon bubble dream

shaped like continents

turning left towards the ocean

leaving the right side behind

in this country they knew

new dreams could come true

untitled #2

there is no river to healing

he sees a long path ahead

with pit stops along the way

it could go on forever

and it can halt whenever you want

but as you walk along

you feel pieces of yourself fading away

pieces

that photos can't put back together

videos only give you so much

even when you keep pressing replay

do you drag this rock of grief with you forever

or do you ripple it away in your puddles of tears

untitled #3

in the temple he rose

as her praying hands stemmed

the rose of her beliefs

the thorns of his

untitled #4

you pulled at my heartstrings

but in the process, it fractured my lungs

my ribs tried to sew the mess

but you wouldn't let me breath on my own

i didn't know the chambers of my heart could unlock

until you ripped through me

and stole the key

untitled #5

it's okay to feel a block in your way. you didn't ruin your only

escape, she did.

untitled #6

as her hand rose

the frigid night pulled her single finger

up to my mouth

trancing it into silence

an afterthought of the summer

reaching into the darkness ahead

to come out the same frozen body of the past

one-foot walks in and two leap out

rolling into the frozen pond

untitled #7

watching boxes tear open

and dinner being served

you swallow your stomach

back down your throat

fruits leave your hand

convinced you're still digesting

dead weight leaves the air

through your skin

out the door

and back to the scale

defying your worth off of

a single number

untitled #8

down to the waterfront

throwing stones

that stay alone

at the bottom

singing all the way down

row your boat

seeing it fly by

above all that is bad

surplus of faces sad

turning around after skipping

sorrows down to ripples

pushing it away

the death of her soul

being taken away

by the weight of stones

ready in hand to

slide down her throat

thinking of tying a string

around the stone

solely connected to her wrist

if thrown down first

will she drown second?

untitled #9

no

is not in her vocabulary

that's why she agreed

to walk the long way

to meet you

she always tried to fill every need

with please

she gave to others

before she gave to herself

starving her soul

to feed others

she'd run miles for you

without even knowing if there's a finish line

you offer the long way to her

and the short to others

because you know that she'll always choose

the one you require her to desire

untitled #10

two solstices' reflecting off

of each other from

cornerstones

of the galaxy

mirrored bodies

for the annual coil of time

shriveled happiness can crumble

and sadness rises while the

moon stays a little bit longer

snow falls off our skin

plucked by the clouds that

stay only a little bit longer

eyelids open to the

same darkness that is within which stays

just a little bit longer

hands reach out filled with warmth to make up for

the frigidness inside

is anyone home?

untitled #11

to rekindle an old flame

is to set up for a wildfire

sightless to understanding

a single match

could lay the world with flames

but you keep a sink

unfilled with water

where to wash the smoke away?

untitled #12

i believe that jellyfish create the waves that form tsunamis

i believe that jellyfish are the stars of the ocean

exploding in slow motion

the ripple of their legs

could cause a colossal

shaking of the earth's core

do jellyfish know that the sky exists?

dear…

dear mother,

the one that is

always there when i need her

to lift my chin up from defeat even

if she's fought a war that day

and to push me forward even

when she's pulling her own weight

i hope that one day

i get to be as strong as you

and in my future

i wish to become as beautiful as you

with arms that reach for every hug

embracing every person

filling them with comfort

eyes that resemble the warmth within your soul

a soul that only knows how to give

to everyone in need of a little bit of love

courageousness and bravery are written

with silk scarves upon your chest

like a badge of honor

every day you teach me to fight

for what i believe in

with a little help from brown girl magic

squeezing our roots so i too

can feel culture bursting through my branches

bestowing the softest brown skin

gentle enough to wash nightmares away

ears ready to listen

and lips always somehow saying the right words

how do you do it all?

i am honored to be your daughter

sharing the same crazy curls and elegant nose

on top of a quaint face and lengthy legs

i am built from you

and i am truly blessed

to have a mother like you

dear sister,

i believe that we are twin flames

not just by blood

but by the same love

and hatred

for the dearest ones around us

i don't believe in luck

because luck found me

coincidences lined up just perfect

neat in row

never too far apart

that our birthdays

fall on the same day every year

a bond like no other

grateful to have you

dear aji,

i can't understand that you're gone

and why the world decided to keep spinning

i miss your stories

and the way i could see your eyes marvel about the past

you lived so many lives that i wasn't there for

i believe that your blood flows through my veins

creating instinctive rhythm as i dance

i hope we meet in another life

so that we can finally dance together again

dear god,

i'm not religious but

god seems pretty cool

    when i think i need him

in times where i don't believe enough in myself

to carry through

i wish i could visit that puppet-controlling master one day

    that's how i think of him

shifting strings above the clouds

granting karma to his greatest detesters

hoping he cuts my string loose

so, i can stop rudely praying to nothing above

reciting heavily

on my knees

greetings to the beginning of the book

hello sweet child

i've enjoyed this drive

where we drove together

oh, how we nosedive

into this random girl's emotions

into the thick and the thin

and look back at the journey

the places we've been

i hope you realize what will occur

and how i am not the enemy

we work hand in hand

like ebony and ivory

you will get there one day

the state of realization

that you are the dawn

of this creation

epilogue

an eye-opening revelation. i wanted this collection to feel like a new lens has reached your eyes. i wanted this collection to make my readers feel a wider sense of visibility. this journey of poetry is long lasting, and i believe that this collection shows my growth as a young writer. there has been pauses along the way, but i am proud of the path that poetry has taken me on. i am honored to share this group of poems, ever so polished and pretty. with this collection, i created content from an outer sense of gratitude and reflection of humanity. i opened my mind to newer beings and feelings. i hope by creating this piece, that others feel inspired to take a look around them and ruminate in the differences of the world.

acknowledgement

to my parents, who have perpetually supported me along this journey of writing and publishing. thank you for never letting go of your grip and being the hands that are always pushing me towards success. to cat mccarrey, for continuing to help me along my journey of poetry, i could have never organized my words without you. thank you to new publishers and people for giving me a chance to share with the world. to mentors through hugo house and seattle youth poet laurette for giving me the ingredients to cook up any poem i can imagine. and lastly, thank you to the people that have brought me here and who have come before me, this is for you.

about the author

Sejal Akerkar

sejal akerkar is a seventeen-year-old senior in high school. born in new york city and after two pit stops in philadelphia and india, sejal has finally made her home in bellevue, washington. this is the author's second poetry collection. as a teenager, she strives to open up the youth eye to past difficulties. she was the proud leadership ambassador for seattle youth poet laurette cohort, a program for youth writers and leaders. she has participated in many acts of service around her community, including teaching poetry to youth, and will continue to purse this passion. she is a growing person trying to feel with others in this drastically altering stage of life as she enters young adulthood. through her collection, she unlocks her personal lens of the world and hopes to explore all living elements.

Made in United States
North Haven, CT
06 November 2022